REALITY
TV
TITANS

ZANY EATS WITH

Andrew Zimmern

Jill C. Wheeler

**Checkerboard
Library**

An Imprint of Abdo Publishing
abdopublishing.com

abdopublishing.com

Published by Abdo Publishing, a division of ABDO, PO Box 398166, Minneapolis, Minnesota 55439.
Copyright © 2016 by Abdo Consulting Group, Inc. International copyrights reserved in all countries.
No part of this book may be reproduced in any form without written permission from the publisher.
Checkerboard Library™ is a trademark and logo of Abdo Publishing.

Printed in the United States of America, North Mankato, Minnesota

062015
092015

 THIS BOOK CONTAINS
RECYCLED MATERIALS

Design: Jen Schoeller, Mighty Media, Inc.
Production: Christa Schneider, Mighty Media, Inc.
Series Editor: Liz Salzmann
Cover Photos: Steve Henke, cover; Alamy, back cover
Interior Photos: AP Images, pp. 19, 20; Corbis, p. 17; Adrian Danciu, pp. 5, 29; Image courtesy of the
Hazelden Betty Ford Foundation, p. 11; Steve Henke, p. 13; Madeleine Hill, p. 23; Mighty Media, Inc.,
p. 27; Shutterstock, pp. 3, 16, 18; The Travel Channel, p. 15; Andrew Zimmern, pp. 6, 7, 8, 9, 21, 25

Library of Congress Cataloging-in-Publication Data

Wheeler, Jill C., 1964-
  Zany eats with Andrew Zimmern / Jill C. Wheeler.
      pages cm. -- (Reality TV titans)
  Includes index.
  ISBN 978-1-62403-822-8
1. Zimmern, Andrew. 2. Cooks--United States--Biography. 3. Food writers--United States--Biography.
I. Title.
  TX649.Z56W44 2016
  641.5092--dc23
  [B]
                    2015005706

CONTENTS

Bizarre Foods

Most people know Andrew Zimmern from the Travel Channel's program *Bizarre Foods with Andrew Zimmern*. On the show, Zimmern eats foods that many people find disgusting. He shows that one person's idea of disgusting may be another person's idea of **delicious**.

Zimmern began as a successful chef. He loved cooking. He also loved travel and learning about other **cultures**. He saw an opportunity to bring the two together. That was the start of his television career.

Today, Zimmern has more than half a million followers on Twitter. He has more than 250,000 fans on Facebook. He has written books, developed food trucks, and made cooking videos. His television program has won several awards. His website has been nominated for the best food website by The Webby Awards.

Zimmern believes food can help bring people together. He uses *Bizarre Foods* to interpret different cultures through their foods. He believes families around the world are a lot alike. They just have different foods on their dinner tables.

Andrew Zimmern's passion for cooking and eating has made him a star.

Foodie in Training

Andrew Scott Zimmern was born July 4, 1961, in New York, New York. His father, Robert, was an advertising executive. His mother, Caren, was a receptionist. He was the couple's only child. When Andrew was six years old, his parents got divorced.

Andrew in his early days of exploring new foods

Robert Zimmern loved traveling, exploring, food **culture**, and of course, eating. He went on many business trips to different cities and countries. Sometimes Andrew went with him. They explored restaurants in Europe and Asia as well as around the United States. Andrew's father encouraged him to eat the local dishes. He tried many different foods.

Andrew was also exposed to fine food at home. His mother studied cooking in California under restaurant owner Victor Bergeron. Bergeron started the Trader Vic's restaurants. She taught Andrew some of the skills she learned.

DID YOU KNOW?
Zimmern has traveled to more than 150 different countries.

Shaky Start

Zimmern attended the Dalton School in New York City. During summer vacations he worked in restaurants on Long Island, New York.

After graduating from Dalton, Zimmern attended Vassar College in Poughkeepsie, New York. He studied art history. But he had become addicted to alcohol and drugs. These addictions plus his classes became too much for Zimmern to manage. After about a year, he dropped out of school.

Zimmern drifted for the next few years. In 1980, he briefly attended the Culinary Institute of America. He cooked in Europe for nine months. He had **internships** in Italy and

Zimmern as a young adult

Early adulthood was filled with
variety for Zimmern. He traveled
often and attended several schools.

France. He cooked for several
months at Hong Kong hotels.

Then he went back to
Vassar. In 1984 he graduated
with degrees in history and
art history. That summer he
worked as a chef at an inn
in Southampton, New York.
Andrew returned to New York
City that fall. His success
as a chef continued. He
helped open and run a dozen
restaurants. By 1990, he was
a partner in a consulting firm.
It focused on **hospitality**.

Bottoming Out

Though achieving some success, Zimmern fell deeper into drug and alcohol addiction. He used drugs during the day. Then he drank alcohol at night. These habits made it hard for him to keep a job.

In his twenties, Zimmern was able to quit using most drugs. However, he could not stop drinking and using **marijuana**. By 1991, Zimmern was unemployed and homeless. He stole to get money for alcohol and food. Zimmern ended up living with other addicts in an abandoned building. It was full of cockroaches and **rodents**.

Finally, Zimmern had had enough. He called a friend and asked for help. Zimmern's friend helped him get into an addiction treatment program. He went to the Hazelden Foundation in Center City, Minnesota. Fortunately, the program was a success. Zimmern stopped drinking and using drugs in early 1992.

After treatment, Zimmern lived in a halfway house in St. Paul, Minnesota. He found a job as a dishwasher at a restaurant called Café Un Deux Trois. It was not long before he was promoted to chef.

Zimmern's time at Hazelden Foundation had a positive influence on his life.

Life in Minnesota

Zimmern spent several years as the head chef at Café Un Deux Trois. Food **critics** praised his work. Customers loved the food too. Then Zimmern became the executive chef at Backstage at Bravo! It opened in 1997. It was a new restaurant and special events center.

After that, he opened his own restaurant. He also started his own company, Food Works, Inc. Zimmern's restaurant never took off, but his career as a celebrity chef did.

Zimmern became a regular on a local television station. He wrote about food for several magazines. In 1999, he taught a class at a cooking school that also had a store. He met Rishia Haas, who was working in the store. He talked her into a date. Then he talked her into a second date. Zimmern and Haas fell in love. They got married in 2002. Their son, Noah, was born in 2005.

DID YOU KNOW?
The Zimmerns live in Edina, Minnesota.

Rishia,
Andrew,
and Noah
Zimmern

A Bizarre Idea

Meanwhile, Zimmern had realized two things. One was that he was happiest working for himself. The other was that was able to see developing food trends. One trend he saw had to do with what are called "fringe foods." These are things most Americans don't think of as normal food. Fringe foods include items such as bugs and animal brains. He wanted to do something with that trend, but he knew he could not do it alone.

Zimmern pulled together a team. It included a talent agent and an entertainment lawyer. They worked with a newswoman from a local television station. They created a new television show. They called it *Bizarre Foods with Andrew Zimmern.*

The ten-minute **pilot** was shot at an elk farm. It was all about eating elk **testicles** and ostrich meat. These are foods most people would consider bizarre!

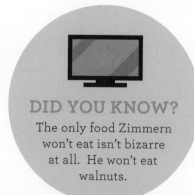

DID YOU KNOW?
The only food Zimmern won't eat isn't bizarre at all. He won't eat walnuts.

Zimmern says he has never gotten sick from the bizarre foods he eats!

Pitching a Winner

Zimmern's team had a **pilot** that was certainly fringe. The next step was to send it to a television network. They sent the pilot to the Travel Channel. Executives at the Travel Channel liked it. They asked Zimmern and his team for three more **episodes**. Each show got strong ratings from Travel Channel viewers. Eventually, Zimmern's team was signed on for six full episodes of *Bizarre Foods*.

The first official *Bizarre Foods* episode aired in February 2007. It quickly won positive reviews from **critics** and viewers. Zimmern was a delightful host. He was at ease in front of a camera. Plus, he had no problem eating **exotic** foods. He tried everything from ant larvae to freeze-dried rotten potatoes to steamed duck embryos. And, he usually said it tasted good!

Larvae are just one super strange food Zimmern has eaten in his travels.

Zimmern's personality shines through on camera and makes him a natural and successful host.

As Bizarre as It Gets

In 2009, *Bizarre Foods* changed to *Andrew Zimmern's Bizarre World*. Food moved off center stage. The show focused on the **cultural** stories behind the food. Unfortunately, it was not as popular as the original show had been. They changed it back to *Bizarre Foods*.

In 2012, Zimmern's team created a new show called *Bizarre Foods America*. The show focused on odd things that Americans eat. Zimmern wanted to show that there were interesting foods at home too. One of them was from his adopted home of Minnesota. It's a Scandinavian dish of dried fish preserved in lye. The dish is called lutefisk.

Eventually, Zimmern returned to the international style of the show. *Bizarre Foods* aired its one hundredth **episode** in 2012.

Lutefisk

Fans around the world love to watch Zimmern try new foods.

Award Winner

Zimmern has received many awards. His online show, *Appetite for Life*, won an Effie award. He has also produced a podcast series called *Go Fork Yourself*. It won a Stitcher award for Food/Cooking Podcast in 2012.

Zimmern has received three James Beard Foundation awards. Zimmern won for TV Food Personality in 2010 and Outstanding Personality/Host in 2013. In 2012, *Bizarre Foods with Andrew Zimmern* won for Television Program on Location.

Winning the James Beard awards was extra special for Zimmern. He had met Beard

James Beard Foundation

James Beard was a famous chef. He also ran a cooking school and wrote more than 20 cookbooks. He advised many prominent chefs. The foundation was started in his memory after he died in 1985.

Rishia and Zimmern celebrate his receiving
a James Beard Foundation award.

when he was a child. Beard was a friend of Zimmern's father. Zimmern
remembers having a meal with his father and Beard when he was
seven. The experience had strengthened his dream of a career in the
food industry.

The AZ Guy

Some people might take it easy with a wildly successful television show. Not Zimmern. He didn't want be just the guy who eats strange foods on TV. He wanted to stay true to his roots as a chef.

So he launched his own food truck in 2012. The Andrew Zimmern's Canteen food truck **debuted** at the Minnesota State Fair. Now there are Andrew Zimmern's Canteen trucks in Florida too. He also opened an Andrew Zimmern's Canteen in Target Field. That's where the Minnesota Twins baseball team plays.

Andrew Zimmern's Canteens offer dishes inspired by his favorite foods discovered on his travels. There are often dishes with goat meat. Goat is the world's most widely consumed red meat. It also has less of an **impact** on the **environment** than many other types of meat.

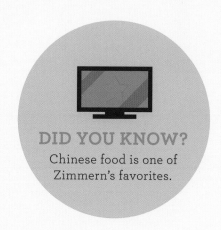

DID YOU KNOW?
Chinese food is one of Zimmern's favorites.

Fans get to interact with Zimmern when he works his Canteen food trucks.

Branching Out

Zimmern didn't stop with his Andrew Zimmern's Canteens. He also has two restaurants at the Minneapolis-St. Paul airport. They are called Minnibar. They offer sandwiches such as Korean sloppy joes and Cubans.

Zimmern did a series of webisodes exploring American food **culture**. He traveled around the United States to do the webisodes. Toyota **sponsored** the series and gave him a Toyota car to use.

Zimmern is also a writer. In 2009, he published a **memoir** titled *The Bizarre Truth*. In 2012, he published a book for young readers. It's called *Andrew Zimmern's Field Guide to Exceptionally Weird, Wild, and Wonderful Foods*. He has written a column for *Mpls.St.Paul* magazine. Delta Air Lines' *Sky* magazine and *Food & Wine* magazine have published articles by Zimmern.

DID YOU KNOW?
Zimmern wants to run for political office once his TV career is over.

Zimmern's not just talented at cooking and eating food, but writing about it too!

Zimmern's website includes original recipes, food articles, interviews, and cooking videos. Zimmern isn't just about food, though. He teaches **entrepreneur** seminars each year at Babson College in Wellesley, Massachusetts.

Weird Is Relative

Zimmern's work shows how alike people around the world are. Even if they seem very different. Everyone has favorite foods. But those foods can vary from country to country.

People in Thailand eat bats. People in England eat blood sausage. They don't think it's unusual. But many people in America probably think it's weird or gross. And people from other countries may think common American foods, such as **processed**-cheese slices, are equally gross! *Bizarre Foods* shows that "weird" often depends on what you're used to.

Zimmern is working on new ideas for shows about food **culture**. He hopes to not travel so much, though. He wants to spend more time with his family. His long-term goal is to scale back. He says he wants to do only 15 things at a time, not 48 things.

It is tough to guess just what the next big food trend will be. However, chances are that Zimmern will be at the front of it!

Sticky Chicken

Serves 2 to 3

Ingredients

- **3 whole chicken wings**
- **2 tablespoons minced ginger**
- **¹⁄₃ cup soy sauce**
- **3 tablespoons oyster sauce**
- **3 tablespoons sugar**

1. Ask an adult for help.

2. Put the wings in a large greased or nonstick frying pan. Cook about 8 minutes over medium heat. Turn the wings after 4 minutes.

3. Turn the heat to medium-low. Add the ginger and cook 1 minute.

4. Mix the soy sauce, oyster sauce, sugar, and ¹⁄₃ cup water in a small bowl. Pour over the chicken. Turn the heat to medium. Cover the pan. Let the chicken simmer for 10 minutes.

5. Uncover the pan. Turn the heat to medium high. Cook 8 minutes, stirring occasionally. The sauce should become thick and sticky.

Timeline

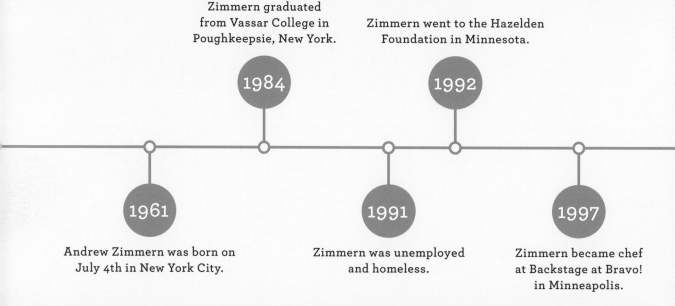

Zimmern graduated from Vassar College in Poughkeepsie, New York.

1984

Zimmern went to the Hazelden Foundation in Minnesota.

1992

1961

Andrew Zimmern was born on July 4th in New York City.

1991

Zimmern was unemployed and homeless.

1997

Zimmern became chef at Backstage at Bravo! in Minneapolis.

Andrew Zimmern Says

"There's nothing more honest than cooking, and when I do it, I can show people what's in my heart."

"Travel is the only place I know of where I am challenged and learn new things."

"Don't eat 'til you're full; eat 'til you're tired."

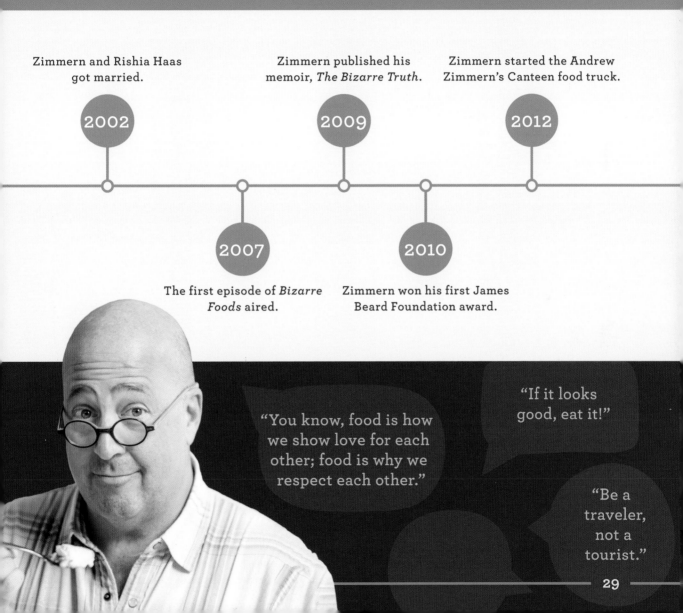

Zimmern and Rishia Haas got married.

2002

Zimmern published his memoir, *The Bizarre Truth*.

2009

Zimmern started the Andrew Zimmern's Canteen food truck.

2012

2007

The first episode of *Bizarre Foods* aired.

2010

Zimmern won his first James Beard Foundation award.

"You know, food is how we show love for each other; food is why we respect each other."

"If it looks good, eat it!"

"Be a traveler, not a tourist."

Glossary

critic – a professional who gives his or her opinion on art, literature, or performances.

culture – the customs, arts, and tools of a nation or a people at a certain time. Something related to culture is cultural.

debut – to make a first appearance.

delicious – very pleasing to taste or smell.

entrepreneur – one who organizes, manages, and accepts the risks of a business or an enterprise.

environment – all the surroundings that affect the growth and well-being of a living thing.

episode – one show in a television series.

exotic – strikingly, excitingly, or mysteriously different or unusual.

hospitality – the business of providing food, drinks, entertainment, and other services.

impact – a strong effect on something.

intern – a student or graduate gaining guided practical experience in a professional field. A person doing this is participating in an internship.

marijuana – an illegal drug made from a certain type of hemp plant.

memoir – a written account of a person's experiences.

pilot – a television episode created as a sample of a proposed series.

process – to change or prepare by special treatment, such as adding coloring, flavoring, or preservatives.

rodent – any of several related animals that have large front teeth for gnawing. Common rodents include mice, squirrels, and beavers.

sponsor – to pay for a program or an activity in return for promoting a product or a brand.

testicle – a part of the male body.

Websites

To learn more about Reality TV Titans, visit **booklinks.abdopublishing.com**. These links are routinely monitored and updated to provide the most current information available.

Index